Baby Sister

Baby Sister

A Promise of Sacrifice

DENNIS STALLINGS

iUniverse

BABY SISTER
A PROMISE OF SACRIFICE

iUniverse books may be ordered through booksellers or by contacting:

iUniverse
1663 Liberty Drive
Bloomington, IN 47403
www.iuniverse.com
844-349-9409

ISBN: 978-1-6632-1610-6 (sc)
ISBN: 978-1-6632-1611-3 (e)

Library of Congress Control Number: 2021900261

Print information available on the last page.

iUniverse rev. date: 01/05/2021

Introduction

On February 3, 2015, my oldest sister, Susie Will Stallings Brooks, died of complications brought on by a stroke. This for me, her baby brother, was a devastating blow in my life. Not even my family members knew at the time how destroyed I was. It was all I could do to compose myself at the funeral. My brother Fred could tell I was struggling with my composure when he leaned over and tapped me on the back. "Are you okay?" he asked softly. I nodded my head, saying I was all right, knowing I was tearing apart inside. Deep within the depth of my emotions and my memories of Susie, I wanted to say something at the funeral, but I realized if I had, I would have been up there for hours rather than the two minutes that were allowed. However, at that moment, God put it on my heart to write this book about the relationship that Susie and I developed through the private and intimate conversations we shared throughout my life as she raised me and three of my brothers.

This book is my way of sharing Susie's legacy with the world because she certainly was the world to me. This book is about her sacrifices, her unconditional love, her promise, her challenges, and the methods that she used to prevent me from failing. This book will explain why she was called Baby Sister. This book will help all the people who knew her to understand why she did what she did the way she did it. This book will put in perspective the reason all my brothers and sisters looked to her for all the answers. Most of all, this book will illuminate the magical bond she and I had from the very first day I lost my biological mother.

Susie Will Stallings Brooks was so much more than a mother, a tremendous second-grade educator, an outstanding wife, and an incredible cook. She was the magnificent woman who, throughout all her achievements, looked back and reached down and pulled my brothers and me from the brink of privation and gave us a life. This book is dedicated to an unselfish untenable woman—a woman we called Baby Sister!

Chapter 1

The Name, the Request, and the Promise

Let me begin in a small town known as Crawford, Mississippi. Susie was the first born to Lonnie Stallings and Sarah Mae Stallings. Following Sarah's separation from Lonnie, she had eight other children fathered by a man named Joseph Brooks. (This man was the cousin of Joe Marshall Brooks, who was the father of Susie's husband, Joe Louis Brooks). The names of the eight children are as follows: Willie, Lucy, MacAuthor, Dorothy, Joseph Jr., Glen, Freddie, and of course, me, Dennis. With every baby my mother had, there was Susie to help change the diapers, cook, and clean up after the babies. Susie was our sister who took care of our mother's babies. This was why my mother and grandmother gave Susie the nickname Baby Sister. This was how we referred to her for the rest of her life. From what I can remember, we lived in a five-room house without an indoor bathroom. This was during the early 1950s and the '60s. Based on the conversations with Susie, I believe the house belonged to our grandmother, whom I never met. When I was about two or three years old, we lost my brother Willie (nicknamed Sonny Boy) in a car accident. By this time, Susie had graduated from Jackson State University and had

1

married Joe Louis Brooks. They had three children: Wanda, who is a month and three days older than I, Romeo, and Monique.

Our mother, Sarah Mae, I was told, was a woman who was always on the go. Whether it was work or play, she loved to get out and about. Often, Susie had to take care of the family while our mother was on the go during those early years. I do remember the evidence of my mother's activities when she took me to Kankakee, Illinois, to see her brother, my uncle George. I was about four or five years old. The one thing I really remember about this trip is that, while I was asleep on the bus, my mother disembarked to go to the restroom at a bus stop. I woke up and ran out of the bus crying. A police officer picked me up and carried me to my mother, who was coming out of the restroom. Yes, my mother was a very outgoing woman. My sister Lucy was the same way. Susie told me that her daughter Monique is just like our mother. She also told me that Monique's daughter, Brooke, carries the same genes. I told Susie that my daughter, Sharita, also has those same traits. Susie would always respond this way: "Dennis, you cannot get rid of our mother's genes. They are here to stay."

When I turned six years old, my mother sent me to school— the first grade. At the time, I just thought school was a place where parents sent their children at six years old. I had no concept of why children went to school. During that school year, I broke my right arm and had to write with my left hand. When my arm healed, I could not write with my right hand anymore. That is how I became left-handed. The only thing I can remember learning the entire year is writing my name. I was truly unaware of what it took to be a good student. At the end of the school year, when I got my report card, I remember running home to my mother telling her that I passed to the second grade. The funny thing about this entire ordeal is that I didn't know if I had passed or not. It wasn't until my mother read it to me. "Promoted to the second grade," she said. You see, what you have to understand is that I could not read well at all. In the second grade, my reading got a little better, but I was quite far behind, and I didn't even realize how bad I was failing.

It was during my second year in school that things began to change in my life. My sister Lucy had move to Flint, Michigan, and this was the year that my mother's health took a turn for the worse. It began with a stroke. My mother still tried to carry on, but the sickness became unbearable for her. One evening, Susie was there at the house along with many other people. I saw a vehicle with red lights on top parked in front of the house. I saw the occupants of that vehicle put my mother on a bed and put her in the vehicle and carry her off. I guess it was about a day later that Susie returned to the house. There were many people there. I was outside in the yard when my sister Dorothy called out to me, "Dennis, Baby Sister wants to see you." I walked into my mother's bedroom slowly. Susie was sitting in a chair surrounded by all my brothers and sisters. "Come here, Dennis," she said. I walked slowly to her and stood next to her. "Dennis, our mother is gone," she said. My tears began to fall, and I put my head in her lap. She picked me up and said, "I want you to know that everything is going to be all right. I am here for you."

You see, this was when Susie began to instill her insight into my life. Susie and I had many conversations about that time. She told me about what happen at the hospital the night our mother died. "Dennis, I remember when our mother was about to die. I was at her bedside, and she took my hand and said, 'Baby Sister, take care of my children.'" Susie responded by saying, "Yes, Mama, I promise I will." Now, I believe at this moment God gave Susie a remarkable gift of strength, courage, and wisdom due to the fact that this was not going to be an easy task at all. And I know I couldn't ever have done anything like that in my lifetime.

During my mother's funeral, I sat next to Susie. We both were crying, and she handed me tissue so I could wipe away my tears. After the funeral, something occurred. I had no clue it had happen until Susie shared it with me in one of our many intimate conversations. She told me that two of our uncles approached her with a solution for the raising of my brothers and sisters. She told me that the two uncles wanted to take me and my brother Fred to live with them. Here is how Susie responded: "Oh no, no, no, no! Now you can take any one of the older brothers, but you are not taking my mother's babies!" This was proof that Susie had so much love for us that she wouldn't risk separating us for anything.

Later, during the 1969 school year, I finished the second grade. I still had no clue about how bad my academics were. I didn't even know how I passed to the third grade. My brother Mack and sister Dorothy were adults, and they had moved to Flint, Michigan, with my sister Lucy. And in the summer of 1969, Susie took Joe Jr., Glen, Fred, and me to Columbus, Mississippi, to start a new life with her and her family. I had no idea what to expect. All I cared about was that someone wanted to take care of us. What I didn't realize was that Susie Will Brooks—Baby Sister—was about to roll up her sleeves and take our mother's request to task and fulfill the promise she'd made to her.

Chapter 2

---※---

A New World

During the summer of 1969, I began to become accustomed to a new way of life in Columbus, Mississippi. Susie brought us into her home and began to make an impact on my life as well as on the lives of my three brothers. One thing you have to remember is that, in Crawford, we had lived such a carefree life. No one taught me much about the simple concepts of daily living; for example, washing your hands after you use the bathroom. In Crawford, I used the bathroom outside mostly. Susie taught us about all the basic grooming practices, especially me. We slept in the back bedroom where there were two sets of bunk beds. The first night she tucked me in on the bottom bunk under my brother Glen. My brother Fred slept in the bottom bunk across from me underneath my brother Joe. Romeo, her son, slept with my brother Glen. Considering where we had been before, yes indeed, this was a new world for us at 2415 21st Avenue, North Columbus, Mississippi.

We met many new people in Columbus, and they became great influences in my life. Susie was very well known in the community. I think it probably was because she was such a great teacher. The other children on the street were so friendly to us when we got there. Instantly we all became close friends and played on that street throughout all those years. We used to play football right in front of our new home. Susie always told me that the reason she didn't mind a bunch children playing in front of her home was that she could see everything that was going on while we were playing. "I have to make sure there wouldn't be any mess," she would say. Besides the new friends we made, I, for the first, time saw and heard an ice cream truck. I also met a mailman who made bird sounds as he delivered the mail.

One of the greatest things I remember about Susie at this time was the fact that she could "burn" in the kitchen. My sister could throw down in the kitchen, and I loved to eat. We all had a special seat at the table. We ate home-cooked meals every day. I could tell Susie really enjoyed cooking for a large family. She truly took pride in her cooking. I later learned it was our grandmother who had taught Susie how to cook and not our mother.

That summer also introduced me to getting new clothes and preparing to start a new school year. I did not like shopping very much, but I did not complain. Just imagine this—Susie carried her three children along with her three brothers in one car; nevertheless, she made it work. I, to this day, don't know how she pulled it off. My older brother Joe did not go with us. I learned later that she helped him until he started working. Now you might think a person could lose it taking all those children shopping, but believe me, Susie had complete control. We understood not to misbehave or she would "splatter us all over that store floor," as she would say. I think she enjoyed dressing her son Romeo and me like twins. As a result, most people thought we were brothers for a long time.

In the fall, the new world in Columbus provided a new school life for me. Susie made one thing perfectly clear to us when she sent us to school: "Do not, under any circumstances, have anyone from that school call me at my job," she firmly said. Then came the quote of my life: "There is only one way to act, and that is the right way," she said. In all the years I was raised by my sister, she made that quote her motto in everything we did or wanted to do. On my first day at school, it didn't take me long to figure something out. Although I was in the third grade, I was behind academically. In my class, which included my niece Wanda, I noticed that there were three groups. The first group were the smart children. The second group were the children in the middle. Then there were the kids in the third group, whose needs were much more challenging. Wanda fell in that first group. I fell into the second group. I knew Susie knew this, but I think she really wanted to see how well I was going to do own my own. As I have stated before in this book, I could not read well when I started in the third grade. After six weeks, I received my first report card. I brought it home to Susie. "Baby Sister, here is my report card," I said. She took it a looked it over. I had two Cs and three Ds. Susie was very, very calm in her response to me. Believe me, this would be the only time she would ever be this calm. "Now, Dennis," she said, "this is not the way. But I am going to show you the way." She spoke calmly. With my grades in mind, Susie knew she had a lot of work to do. She knew that, if she was going to fulfill the promise she had made to our mother, she was going to start by not allowing me, the youngest of the four brothers, to fail.

At that point, all I can remember is Susie bringing down four imaginary walls all around me. This was the moment when I realized that Susie was about take on one of the most challenging ventures in her life. For this was when she set out to transform an eight-year-old boy who could barely read his own name into a straight-A student. This new world was also about to reveal to me the real Susie Will Stallings Brooks—the one true Baby Sister.

Chapter 3

The Rules and the Rants

As I have implied before, Susie was in total control of her family, especially my brothers and me. There was no disrespecting Susie or her husband, Joe. It was always, "Yes, Baby Sister. No, Baby Sister." Each one of us had our personal encounters and experiences that she helped us with. But I think it was the rules Susie put in place in the home of eight children that made the difference. I remember telling some of my classmates about some of the rules I had to follow. "How can you live like that?" "I would just leave!" These are examples of the responses I would get. I often wondered why Susie had such strict rules while raising us. It wasn't until I was a grown man that she gave me the answer. I told Susie that I would not raise my children the way she raised us. "Well, Dennis," she said, "I understand that, but what you have to know is that I don't know if the way I raised y'all was right or wrong. All I know is I had to *try*!" You see, Susie did everything she could to protect us as well as her own children. The amazing thing about this was the fact that she gave up some of the enjoyable things with her own children in order to raise her brothers. I believe that Susie would not have put the rules in place if the four of us had not been there. Her love for us made her sacrifice the special moments of a normal family. This is what made her such a magnificent woman, and this is why we loved her so much.

Susie put stringent rules in the home for two reasons. First, it was for our personal protection from any circumstances that might harm us. Second, it was to eliminate any distraction from our schoolwork. Susie never wanted anything to be an excuse for us not to learn and get our homework done and done properly. Due to the fact that we were already behind in several areas of our education, Susie knew that she had to prevent any and all distractions whatever way she could.

No one could go outside and play on school days. That was one of the first rules I remember. This meant that, when we got home from school, we stayed in the house until it was time to go to school the next day. If anyone of us asked to go outside or to go anywhere, the answer was the same each time: "No! Go somewhere, sit down, get a book in your hand, and read!" Now sometimes this hurt because, if our friends were outside playing in the street, we wanted to play also, but Susie never wavered in her quest to improve our reading and our grades. As far as she was concerned, playing outside on a school day was a huge distraction. Trust me, I got used to it. Not only that, my reading and my grades did slowly, over time, improve.

The next rule probably got to me more than it did to anyone else in the house. We could not watch any television on school nights. Imagine, Monday through Thursday, no TV. I loved to watch TV. In Crawford, we hadn't had an inside bathroom, but we did have a television. When my friends at school asked me if I'd seen a certain television show, I would just respond this way; "Man, I missed that show! Tell me about!" Susie would make some exceptions if—and only if—the TV show was an assignment for school. I remember reading the same book over and over just to make the time go by without television. I also listened to a great deal of radio and music. I would also make up imaginary games to play by myself. When I was nine years old and bored, I was alone in the bedroom one evening after dinner. I decided to gather together about four of my brothers' belts. I connected them together to make one long belt. After I had the finished product, I had to try it out. I stretched my long invention behind me holding the end of it in my hand. I swung it over my head as if I was throwing a fishing rod. That's when it happened. The hard belt buckle at the end of my invention hit the glass light cover on the ceiling. The light cover hit the floor with a loud *crash*! Everyone came running down the hall with Susie leading the pack. All I could here was everyone yelling "Baby Sister, what's going on?" Susie burst open the door, and there I was standing there, glass all over the floor, with this dumbfounded look on my face. Susie didn't say one word. She quietly took my long belt invention from me, folded it in half, and wore me out. It was the longest spanking! I thought it would never end. After my older brother Glen cleaned up the glass, I went to bed crying. I didn't realize it at the time, but when I got older, I came to the conclusion that Susie had been so right. If I had only, at the time, been somewhere sitting with a book in my hand reading, that incident wouldn't have happened. It was tough, but eventually I got used to all the rules. Of course, my schoolwork continued to improve, and I decided not to make any more inventions.

Susie also placed into effect curfew rules. I was too young to challenge this rule, but my brother Fred, who was nicknamed Curly because of his hair, was a different story. The first time Fred violated this rule, Susie told him that she would not open the door. Fred was late once again. Susie stood at the front door yelling at him. "I am *not* opening this door. Go back to where you came from!" she yelled. Susie went on yelling and yelling at the front door. Finally, Susie stopped yelling. She then heard laughing coming from our bedroom. She slowly walked down the hall and opened the door. Romeo and I were laughing like hyenas. Fred had left the front door, walked to the back bedroom window, and climbed through. He'd climbed into his bed and was fast asleep. "Curly!" she yelled. "Yes, Baby Sister," he said softly. "Don't you come to this house this late anymore. Next time I will lock all my doors and windows!" she said firmly, and she walked out of the room. I heard her telling Joe that she could not believe that boy got through the window and into bed where he was sleeping. Of course, all of us in the bedroom continued to laugh. Well, Fred did challenge Susie once again. This time there were no windows unlocked for him to climb through. Fred knocked on the front door. Susie stood firmly at that front door and said, "I don't know where you are coming from, but, Curly, you need to go back to where it is because I am not opening this door." Then what Fred said next made Susie's heart melt: "Baby Sister, I don't have anywhere else to go." Susie, with tears in her eyes, quietly open the door. You see, with Susie it was all about the love she had for each one of her brothers. And that was the true purpose of all those rules.

Susie expected to get results from her tough rules. However, she didn't take anything for granted, especially when it came to our education. I have to admit that, during my elementary school years, I was always nervous about receiving my report card every six week. Susie demanded good grades from us as well as from her own children. Every six weeks, when report cards came out, the day was what I like to call Judgement Day. Susie would line us up in a straight line. She would have her belt or strap on her arm ready for spanking. She would have each one of us step forward and present his or her report card. Those who had a good report card, stepped to the right. Those who had a bad report card, stepped to the left. I don't have to tell you what would happen to those of us who fell on that left side. Yes, sometimes I was on that left side. Susie could deal with Cs, but Ds and Fs were totally unacceptable. Even then, she would accept only so many Cs. Susie knew that, if we were going to be successful in life, we had to do well in school. Due to the fact that she was one of the greatest second-grade teachers, she saw first-hand what would become of children who didn't get a good education and make good grades. I cannot tell you if the way Susie did this was right or wrong. All I know is that, for me, it was effective. Today, I am so grateful for what she did and the way she did it. Due to this and all the other rules Susie place upon us, I became a student who not only wanted to do well, but a student who finally got the drive to do well.

Even with strict rules in place, raising eight children can take a toll on a parent. Susie was no different. There came a time when she had to let off a little steam. Susie did this every Sunday morning. This went on throughout my elementary school years. I called them the Sunday Morning Rants. One unusual thing about these rants was that they never included her own children. They were all about our mother and the eight children she had. The other unusual thing was that they only involved sticking to the rules and staying out of the streets. This was about my older brothers who were the only ones who could be out in the streets anyway. I don't know why Susie chose Sunday to shout these rants. However, I think it was because all of us were in the house and she had the audience she needed. I can't speak for everyone else, although I know they heard her, but I listened and heard every word.

On a typical Sunday morning, as we were all in bed, hours before we went to church, Susie would get up quietly and walk up the hall to the kitchen to start breakfast. I will never forget that walk up the hallway. She wore house shoes like flip-flops. As she walked up the hall, we could hear nothing but that sound her house shoes would make: flip-flop, flip-flop, flip-flop. After that, we would smell the bacon or sausage cooking. Then, suddenly, out of nowhere it would start: "'I don't understand that woman,' the people in Crawford used to say," she would yell. "'Why is that woman having all those babies?'" I would lie in bed quietly listening to the rants that questioned my mother and her children, which included me of course. I can't remember the exact wording, but her rant started with this subject then moved from subject to subject all about our mother and her eight children. I kept wondering why people would talk about my mother that way. The rants concluded with Susie making a very conflicting statement: *"I can't wait for you all to get out of my house!"* She would conclude. I would feel so bad about these rants each and every Sunday when they went down. The other unusual thing about these rants was what followed. I guess it was how Susie was letting us know it was time to get up. After the yelling stopped, we could hear the sound of her house shoes as she came back down the hall. She would stop at our bedroom door. Then, with a loud burst, the door would come flying open. "Get up! Get up and get my room clean!" she would yell forcefully. All of us would scatter like roaches. She would turn to leave, but then she'd turn back to our room. "What is that *odor?* There is an odor in here! Get my room clean now!" Then she'd walk away back up to the kitchen. At that time, all of us would just breathe a sigh of relief. I could never figure out what that odor was, but I guess a room where five boys lived would certainly reek with some unpleasant odors.

As an adult, I asked Susie this question in one of our private conversations. "Baby Sister, why did you tell us when we were little about how people talked about our mother?" I asked. "Dennis," she said, "the people of Crawford knew our family quite well. They knew how outgoing our mother was. So they all just kept wondering why she was having children when there was no one to help her but me. Well, I wanted all of you to know how difficult it was for me and our mother to take care of all the babies. What you have to understand is that, most of the time, there was no one else to look after all of you but me." After she finished speaking, my heart went out to her. For the first time, I finally understood all the rants. For so long, Susie had been taking care of us, and I didn't even know it until she shared her experiences with me. I finally understood why all the rules were in place. Susie had taken care of us for so long, she had grown attached to us more than our very own mother had. In addition to this, there was an agape love for us that no one except me and my brothers would ever understand.

Chapter 4

Reading is the Answer

For a very young woman, Susie was incredibly gifted in developing students' ability to learn. The basis for all this was reading. Susie believed that if a student could read, he or she could master any subject. Throughout some of our intimate conversations, Susie explained to me her philosophy on education. She believed all students could be taught if they were willing to learn. The problem was twofold: the ability of the student and the parents' involvement in the child's education. She could not understand why some parents would not help their children in the education process. You see, the reason I am pointing this out to you is this: My first report card was horrible. I could not read well in the third grade. As a result, Susie's involvement in my education was profoundly adamant. People may think that some of Susie's tactics for getting results out of me and my three brothers were unorthodox, but they were truly effective. Now, I am about to tell you what Susie did for me to help me conquer and master the education process. The answer was simple: *"Read!"*

I sat at the kitchen table as Susie began to help me with my third-grade reading assignment. Her daughter Wanda sat next to me. I always envied Wanda because she could read so well. When she read, the words flowed so smoothly, they sounded like a sweet music melody. Oh, how I wished I could read like that.

Susie pulled up a chair next to me and sat with a black strap in her hand. "Read, Dennis," she said softly.

"Yes, Baby Sister," I responded. I began to read out loud very slowly. I stumbled through the sentences with breaks in between words. When I came upon a word I didn't know, I would stop.

"Dennis, sound the word out," Susie instructed. I tried, but I could not quite get it. Then she sounded it out for me, breaking it down into syllables and saying the word. I pronounced the word and kept reading. I made the mistake of trying to memorize words instead of sounding them out as she wanted. When I would come to the same word again and could not remember what it was, *whop!* was the sound of black strap hitting me on my lap. "Dennis, you have to break down the word and sound it out," she said firmly. That's how it went for me that night. All I could think about was, *Will this night ever end?* Susie knew that, in order to bring me up to speed with reading and all my other subjects, she had to use any means necessary to make sure I did not fail in school.

Throughout the years, as Susie raised her four brothers along with her own children, each one of my brothers had a different experience. Susie knew us so well, and she knew how to deal with each one of us individually. This is what made her so special to me and my brothers.

Throughout the third grade, my reading got better and better. My grades came up some, but they were far from Susie's standards. I remember her putting it like this: "A C means you're clumsy, a D means you're dumb, and an F means you are a fool. You don't have to go to school to be a fool." That was also the first time that I heard her use this statement: "Go somewhere, sit down, get a book in your hand, and read!" This statement became her trademark. She used it to get us to behave or when we wanted to go somewhere that she highly disapproved of. Susie always told me that you cannot get into trouble if you are somewhere sitting down with a book in your hand. If you think about it, she was ever so right. Susie had the answer to most of the problems our youth are facing today. The answer is simple: *Read!*

Chapter 5

The Anchor—The Glue

Susie was a master at solving problems that my three brothers and I encountered on a daily basis. However, the amazing thing about her problem solving skills was how she also remedied solutions for my other older brothers and sisters who lived in Flint, Michigan. It didn't matter what the problem was with my siblings. The moment chaos started, the phone call to Susie was made.

As I sat in the little old rocking chair, I listened to Susie manage and solve the unthinkable problems that concerned my brothers and sisters. I thought it was somewhat strange that grown people who had their own lives and, in some cases, families, would be calling Susie to solve their problems. Nevertheless, it happen all the time because they all looked to Susie as the mother figure she had always been. What people have to understand is that Susie was always the anchor that held our family in place so we wouldn't run adrift. She was the glue that held the family in place so we wouldn't fall apart. This is who Baby Sister was and will always be to us.

Whether it was my two sisters, Dorothy and Lucy, or my three brothers Mack, Joe Jr., and Glen, Susie handle problems with firm grace and love. I can't recall all the details of the problems, but I know it was always a family situation with their family or a problem among them. I do recall one problem Joe Jr. had with my sister Lucy. Apparently, Lucy had borrowed money from Joe. As everyone knows, loaning money between siblings can lead to chaos. Joe had a difficult time getting Lucy to pay him back. So, who did he call? The one person who could remedy the situation: Baby Sister. Susie made that call, and Joe got his money back. This is just one example of Susie holding all of them together. This went on year after year. Every problem was run by Susie either for a solution or an approval.

In my private conversations with her, she also expressed to me the importance of taking care of each one of us. She told me how she would send money to my brother Glen when he was going through a rough time. She would tell me to pray for Dorothy who suffered with mental problems. When we lost my brother Mack to cancer, she got us all there to the funeral. It was a never-ending process for Susie to hold our family together. She did it all the way up until she died. Make no mistake about it: my mother's eight children would have run adrift and fallen apart if it hadn't been for the *anchor* and the *glue* we called Baby Sister.

Chapter 6

The Bond

Of the eight children my mother had, I was probably the height of Susie's success as she completed the promise she made to our mother. I know it was because I was the youngest of the eight. Susie knew that she could not allow me, of all the children, to fail in school and in life. She knew she had to give me a solid foundation. I have shared how I started out in the third grade and couldn't read well and how she helped me through that. I want to share with you now how we developed a most special bond. It was so much more than a mother-son relationship. Susie's greatest work was me, and I always thanked her up until she died for giving me the opportunity to have a life. Our relationship was so much more than anything else in my life. We had a bond that people of Columbus talked about, especially all Susie's friends and educators in the community. Because of our bond, I received aid from so many of Susie's friends.

Before I get into this chapter, I want all Susie's friends who are still here and may be reading this book to know how much I love you all. You all know who you are.

My elementary years in school were up and down, but I always improved from year to year. Susie continued to put the hammer down to help me understand that nothing was more important than a good education. As I grew, Susie taught me about other things that helped me understand life, and this included integrity. I remember one incident in which I learned that lying was not a good solution. Susie and Joe were out on one particular day, and I was looking in the refrigerator for something to eat. I had to move some things around to get to whatever it was I was trying to get. I accidentally knocked down a glass bowl of black-eyed peas. There was a crash, and glass was everywhere. In the process of cleaning it up, I cut my hand. Everyone knew what I had done, but they said not word when Susie, who was so upset, asked me what had happened. I hated seeing Susie upset, so unwisely, I lied. "Dennis," she said, "how did you cut your hand?" "Baby Sister, I was looking in the refrigerator, and when I closed the door, I cut my hand on the door," I said as I stumbled over my words. No one else said anything. They all knew I was lying, including Susie. Later, at the dinner table, I noticed Susie was still upset, and that made me sick to my stomach. Then Susie, like a criminal lawyer, went to the refrigerator. She opened the door and then she slammed it shut. "I don't understand what happened to my peas!" she yelled. "I was thinking about having my peas to eat when I got home." Then my brother Glen testified. "That is what Dennis broke—the glass bowl with the peas in it." Susie yelled, "Dennis, come here! Why did you lie to me?" "Baby Sister," I said with tears raining down my face, "I just did not want you to get upset." "Dennis, I am not upset about you breaking the glass bowl of peas. I'm upset because you cut your hand." For first time, I understood two things: Never lie to Baby Sister. And Susie held caring love for me and my safety. Susie always told all of us that, if we lied, we would steal, and if we stole, we would kill. None of that was good. Susie lived her life making sure that my brothers and I understood that.

Another thing Susie taught me as we bonded had to do with money and work. When it came to taking care of my money, I was horrible. I didn't always have very much growing up, but what little I got, I blew. I could never remember what I spent it on when Susie asked me. I once obtained about $400 over the course of the summer. Susie did not take it from me. Instead, in order to teach me how important money was, she kept track of my money in her head as she took me shopping. At each store she would say, "Dennis, it's time for you to get yourself some sneakers." I would purchase the sneakers. She did that with all the things I needed for the next school year. When I ran out of money, she knew it, and she knew exactly what I had bought with. At the time, I did not understand, but when I got older, the concept was obvious. Susie helped me to understand that money was for needs first other things second. From that point on, whenever I earned some money, I would talk to her about what I needed to buy first to make sure she was in agreement with me. I knew I could never go wrong with her guiding me along.

When it came to work, everyone in the house benefited from her revelations. On Saturdays, we had what I now like to call Field Day. This is a term I got from my tour in the US Navy. It consisted of detail cleaning all spaces. Susie assigned each of us jobs. We did it all—cleaning windows and floors as well as doing laundry and dishes. One Saturday, one of Susie's friends came by. Susie and Joe had gone out, but we were all busy cleaning. Susie's friend was so impressed with the organizational structure of the work, she couldn't wait to call Susie that evening to tell her. Throughout my youth, Susie used every aspect of cleaning the home to teach us good work ethics until we all started working real jobs.

During some summers, Susie would take us all down to Crawford to work in a garden that we had at her husband's parents' home. I hated this endeavor, but it did teach me about hard work. Besides, our labors produced much-need vegetables, which we planted, cared for, harvested, and cleaned. It also made me want to do well in school because I did not want to farm for a living. Nevertheless, Susie knew three things this work would do. First, it would bond us as a family. Second, it would teach us great work skills. Third, it would keep us out of trouble. I have to admit that it work for me and my brothers as well as her own children.

Despite all the things Susie taught me, our bond didn't blossom until I reached the seventh grade in school. This was when Susie really began to see the fruits of her labor. I became so close to Susie, and ironically, it all resulted from my success in education. When I started the seventh grade, I was placed in a reading class despite the fact that I could read. I guess it was because of the standardized testing I had taken in the sixth grade. Nevertheless, after the first six weeks, I received my report card and discovered I needed only one more point to make the honor roll! Susie was surprised and ecstatic. Over the next six weeks, I made straight As. When my name appeared in the newspaper's honor roll listing, Susie was so proud. She had bounce and a kick in her step from all her excitement. Her friends all around Columbus were calling her about my success. Susie told them that she knew that I hadn't had a good start in school when I was in Crawford. She told them that I probably just had to get used to a new school system. I heard her all night talking to friends about me. I had never seen Susie like that before. The next week, when I went to school and walked into my home room, my teacher called me up and said something that shocked me right out my socks: "Dennis, this is your new schedule. Your classes are changing." "Why?" I asked. "Well, let me put it this way: You are no longer taking a reading class," she explained. I was still confused until I got home and told Susie what had happened. "Baby Sister, they changed my schedule at school," I said with a confused look on my face. "I know," she responded. "I called the school system and had your schedule changed." I found out later that Susie did not like the fact that I was making straight As *and* taking a reading class. I could not believe what she had done. Susie cared more about my education than anything. This was a major milestone for me, and it began a new relationship with my sister, a relationship that made Susie get tougher on me rather than not easier. Once I started making all As, Susie would not accept anything below a B. She begin to hold me to a higher standard, even more than she held my brothers. I know this because, in my world history class, I slipped on a test and made a grade of 78 percent. The teacher, who knew Susie, called her and told her my result. Susie fussed me out so bad I thought I was going to fall apart. My brother Fred heard all this and asked me what I had made on the test. When I told him, he yelled, "Man, if I got a seventy-eight, I would be a happy boy!" At that point, I knew Susie had a higher standard for me.

My educational success brought about a domestic bond with Susie also. During this particular bonding, she shared with me some of her best-kept secrets. The most influential one was her special recipes as she began to bring me into the world of cooking in the kitchen. It all started on Sunday mornings when I began to get up with Susie to help her with breakfast. She provided detailed instructions on everything from using the right pans and utensils to taking out all the necessary ingredients before beginning. Then she would talk me through on every procedure as we cooked eggs, bacon, sausage, grits, and toast. "Dennis," she instructed, "you must keep turning the bacon evenly and slowly because it will burn if you don't. You don't want to cut the sausage too thick. This makes it easy to cook through thoroughly. Grits have to cook over low heat to make sure they are not gritty." Her cooking instructions were always very detailed. After a few weeks of instruction, I would get up before Susie and have all the breakfast for the entire family prepared by the time she entered the kitchen.

On our next bonding venture in the kitchen, Susie began to teach me to bake. My first project was called Sock-It-to-Me Cake. For me, this required elevated cooking skills, but Susie was right there with me every step of the way. "Dennis," she advised, "you must make sure you mix all the ingredients until there aren't any lumps." It took me a few cakes before I mastered the project on my own, but I got so good at it that Susie allowed me to make a cake any time I wanted to. Susie also shared cooking lessons with me as I learned how to make cornbread, pound cake, and sweet potato pie. Susie then shared with me something that she had never shared with anyone else including her own children. She reached in the back of the cabinet and pulled out her green recipe box.

"Dennis," she said with great secrecy, "this box contains a lot of my recipes, but you must never take this box away from the kitchen. Do you understand?"

"Yes, Baby Sister, I do," I responded.

The box contained some of the most outstanding dishes, and I wanted very much to take that box with when I left home. However, Susie would not allow it. Instead, I had to call her all the time to ask her for instructions for certain dishes I was trying for the first time. This kept our cooking bond ever so close. Not only did Susie teach how to master dishes in the kitchen, she also taught me how to master the BBQ grill. I learned how to correctly season and prepare meats, how start the charcoal, and when to place the meats on the grill. Everything was so detailed with her. Susie once told me why she wanted to learn to cook. "Dennis," she said, "if you never get married, at least you will know how to cook for yourself." I understood that, but I didn't count on falling in love with cooking, which, to me, meant becoming a master in the kitchen. To this day, I love being in charge of my kitchen. Here's what Susie told my wife, Sharon: "Sharon, if he wants to be in charge of the kitchen, step back and let him." I think of all the bonding Susie and I shared, cooking was the most enjoyable. Those times are what I will miss about her the most.

Holding me to a higher standard, teaching me how to maneuver around the kitchen, and teaching me attention to detail—these are what our bond was all about and made our bond so special. These experiences are what I loved about my sister, Susie. Her sacrifices brought me from a child who could barely read to a student who got straight As as well as a guy who is a great cook, a graduate of Mississippi State University, a naval officer, and a successful businessman. No one else in our family had a meaningful bond like the one I had with Susie. She was my love, my rock to lean on, and my inspiration. She was an incredible woman, and we called her Baby Sister.

Chapter 7

—✤—

True Feelings in Departing

Throughout the process of being raised by Susie, there were three things she always drilled in us: get a good education, get a job, and *get out of her house!* At the time, I thought she was totally serious about that third one, but then my oldest brother Joseph Jr. put it to the test.

Joe Jr. helped Susie a lot. Because he was the oldest, he kept us in line and watched us when Susie and her husband, Joe, were gone. Joe Jr. apparently did quite well in school despite the fact that he worked a job the entire time he attended school. Joe Jr. graduated from high school in 1972. That summer he went to Susie with a decision he had made. "Baby Sister," he said, "I have decided to move to Flint, Michigan, to live with Mack, Lucy, and Dorothy." "No!" Susie responded. "I have just got all the paper work together you need to go to college." Nevertheless, Joe Jr. had made up his mind to leave. Later that summer, Joe Jr. was packing his bags and putting them in the trunk of the car. I was standing next to Susie. I glanced up at Susie and saw a confusing sight. Her hand was balled up in a fist. As she held her hand against her chin, tears were running down her face like a hard rain. I quickly ran in the house to my brother Fred. "Curly!" I yelled. "Why is Baby Sister crying? She always told us to get out of her house."

Yes, this was the first test that brought out Susie's true feelings for me and my brothers.

I thought at the time that it maybe was all about my brother Joe leaving until a few years later when it came to my brother Glen. Of the four of us, Glen was the weakest in school, but Susie helped him get through it all. Susie always told Glen that he needed more skills for the work force to give him more options in life. Following school, Glen got a job at Fred's Department Store. They moved him around a lot, but he was never too far from home. I don't know how Susie knew this, but she told Glen that he would lose this job, and after a year or so he did. That's when he decide to leave for Flint to be with my other brothers and sisters. Susie hated the idea because she wanted Glen to go to trade school to get more skills. Later that year, I found myself standing next to Susie again while Glen was packing his bags and putting them in the car. She displayed the same look as her tears fell hard. I just didn't understand why all these true feeling were coming out at that time.

It wasn't until I was a grown man when Susie answered that question in one of our intimate conversations. That was when she shared with me the promise she had made to our mother about taking care of us. She told me the reason she had cried about Joe Jr. and Glen leaving. "Dennis, I didn't want Jr. to leave because I knew that he had the chance to go to college. He would have been the second one of us to go. I just hated to see him pass up that opportunity." As she spoke to me, her tears began to fall. She continued about Glen as the tears got heavier. "As for Glen, I knew what needed to do. I begged him to go to a trade school. I just wanted him to better equipped for life." That's when I realized that her "get out of her house" wish did not reflect her true feelings at all. Susie just wanted the very best for us, and she didn't want us to make any wrong choices. She admitted to me that it was just the "mother" in her that did not want us to take a wrong turn. I think it was due to the love she had for our mother and the promise she had made to her.

Things were somewhat different when it came to my brother Fred. Fred had been working at different jobs since he was thirteen years old. So the job part of life he had down better any of us. However, Susie wanted him to go to college anyway. In 1978, after he graduated from high school, Susie set him up to attend her alma mater, Jackson State University. This made Susie a very happy women. Little did she know that the one thing she had drilled into us about getting a job would end the dream of Fred completing his college education. In fact, he barely got his education started. Following one semester of college, Fred got not only one job, but two, and quit school. Susie was fine with this because this has been Fred's "thing" all during his youth. He stayed right there in Jackson where he is today. He always came home so he never gave Susie a chance to shed those tears. Susie told me that, as long as Fred was working and happy, she was happy.

As for me, there was only one thing Susie had in mind, and that was for me to go to Mississippi State University. After I graduated from high school, Susie got me into Mississippi State's summer program. My second semester there, I slacked off on my grades, and Susie made it perfectly clear to me: I had to either get it together or drop out. That was all the motivation I needed from her. Overall, I think my four years at MSU were probably the best years of my life. As a matter of fact, I was having so much fun I was caught off guard when Susie received a letter from the dean of education and marketing stating that I only needed two more classes to graduate. Just like that, my collegiate career was over. Susie had achieved her final goal in fulfilling the promise to our mom. She was such a proud woman when I graduated. She was on cloud ten, but I was not satisfied at all.

One of the most difficult times of my life happened right after I graduated from college. I had a degree in marketing and education, but I did not want to teach. So I took the business route when I began looking for a job. That was frustrating for me. I was angry because I knew this world had more to offer me than what was in Mississippi. I probably would have not been successful then if it hadn't been for the encouragement Susie gave me. A recruiting officer from the US Navy had called the house to speak to me about joining. I did not want to go into the navy. Susie, at this point, sat me down and said, "Dennis, I think you need to give the military a chance. They can help you." I thought about it for a while, and I came to the conclusion that maybe Susie was right. At least, the military would get me out of Mississippi. To this day, I thank Susie for that advice because going into the navy was the smartest move I ever made. I will never forget going to my first job in San Diego, California. Susie looked at me as I was getting ready to leave. Her eyes were beginning to water. I quickly jumped in her face and said, "Oh, no, no, no! Don't you even start that crying on me! This is my job, and this is what you trained me for." She smiled and dried her eyes.

While in the navy, I graduated from Officer Candidate School, another proud day for Susie. Throughout my four more years of the navy, Susie continue to advise me about almost everything, from places and people to see to different recipes for dishes to prepare. There was no problem big or small that she couldn't help me with. She was always right there for me no matter what stage of my life I was in.

In April 1990, following my tour in the navy and my acceptance of a corporate job in Atlanta, Georgia, I returned home to prepare to leave home and Mississippi for good. That was a day that I think Susie did not want to see at all. Despite all the success she had enjoyed in developing me for the world, she still dreaded my leaving. I stood there next to my car in the driveway. It was just the two of us. This was the moment that Susie told me something that she had never told anyone, not even her own children, and it blew me away. "Dennis, you don't have to leave." "What do you mean, Baby Sister?" I asked. At this point, Susie was as serious as I had ever seen her. "I mean you don't have to go anywhere. We can put a trailer for in the backyard, and you can just stay here." "Baby Sister," I said, "you have made a life for me, and I thank you so much. I love you and Joe for what you have done for me, but I must go and live my own life. A life that you have prepared me for." As I was speaking, the tears began to fall like water from a faucet. She nodded her head and said that she understood. As I drove off, I could see her in the rearview mirror as she stood at the edge of the driveway in heavy tears. There she stood until my car turned the corner.

No matter how much Susie yelled at us about getting out of her house, her true feelings were for us to be successful but not to ever leave. The promise she had made to our mother had an attachment effect that she found hard to overcome. It all came out as we each departed her home. It was more than just a motherly instinct because of the sacrifice she had made just for me and my three brothers. This is why Susie Will Stallings Brooks was a great and remarkable woman.

Chapter 8

Wanda, Rome, and Monique

If anyone was under the impression that Susie, while putting a great deal of focus on me and my three brothers, somehow neglected her own children, they were highly mistaken. Before we got there, Susie had involved her children very much in the things that she wanted for them. That trend continued even after my brothers and I arrived. As I stated earlier in this book, Susie did not put the tough rules in place until we arrived. The rules were for our benefit, but her children were enhanced by them as well. Susie's highest traits were instilled and carried on by her children. Because of their unselfish characteristics, Susie's children had nothing but love for us. They treated us as if we were their very own biological brothers. As a matter of fact, we were such a close-knit family, most people thought we were all brothers and sisters anyway. During the course of my adult life, I was fortunate to sit with Susie and listen to her speak about Wanda, Rome, and Monique in the most delicate ways.

Wanda Jean Brooks has always been the standard that I have always tried to pattern myself after since we started the third grade together. Susie was always proud of how Wanda could read. I used to just listen to her read. All that was needed was music because the words flowed together ever so smoothly. Susie also introduced Wanda and Monique to music through piano lessons.

She also had Wanda taking ballet lessons among many other things. Susie was never surprised at Wanda's success in school and other activities because she expected it from her children.

Wanda was always the person I would go to get the information about what was going on in the house with family. For example, she always knew what I was getting for Christmas or who was coming to visit. Trust me, if I wanted to know something, Wanda was always the source. As an adult, I am the only one who calls her by her middle name, Jean. It's just a thing that shows our close connection to each other. While I was sitting with Susie one day, She told me two things that Wanda did that had taken her by surprise. I have to admit it took me by surprise also because I had no idea it happened the way Susie told me. I was telling Susie how amazing it was for Wanda and me to graduate from high school together and go to Mississippi State together also. "Yes it was, Dennis," Susie responded. "But Wanda was not supposed to go to Mississippi State with you." "What!" I said, in shock. "Oh, no, Dennis. I had Wanda set up to go to Jackson State," Susie began to tell me. "When I took you to get set up at Mississippi State, Wanda was just going with me for the ride. And when the administrator finished with you, she looked at Wanda and said, 'Okay, Mrs. Brooks. Dennis is done. Wanda, are you ready?' And Wanda said, 'Yes.' I had this strange look on my face because I was in total shock." As for me, I had always thought that Wanda was going to MSU with me. Susie and I laughed for long time when she shared that story with me. The next time I was surprised was when I came home in between duty stations in the navy. Wanda had her degree in education and had been teaching West Point, Mississippi, that past year. I was sitting talking to Susie and telling her that Wanda told me that she was going to Houston, Texas, to visit some classmates. "Dennis," she said, "Wanda called me from Texas and said, 'Mom, I found a job, and I'm not coming back.' Dennis, I was just shocked, but all I could say was okay." I was rolling in laughter. Wanda also got married and lives in Texas today. I am very impressed with Wanda because she graduated from MSU in three years and continued on to earn her master's in counseling. She actually followed in Susie's footsteps, which was nothing less than Susie expected. It was a true mother-daughter success story if I must say so myself.

Although Wanda and I were the same age and in the same grade in school, Romeo was the one whom I spent most of my childhood playing with. Romeo Brooks, alias "Sweet Rome," alias "Casanova," was the child who knew everyone and loved to talk to people. He was really just like his father. When I sat down with Susie, she put like this: "When Rome was little, he used to go outside. If there was no one out there, Rome would make a lot noise until some other children came outside too. I don't know why I didn't name him Joe after his father because he is just like Joe." What impressed me about Rome was that, when he was seven and eight years old, he could identify any year, make, and model of car no matter where he saw it. I used to ask him how he could tell what each was. "Dennis," he told me, "You can tell by the headlights or the shape of the bumper." Rome was also a great tennis player in high school, and he was also great in the marching band. After high school, Rome attended Rust College. I had come home from Mississippi State, and Rome walked in from Rust. Susie was sitting at the kitchen table, and Joe was standing in the hallway. "Okay!" Rome began to yell. "I need some money. I know you got it, so give it up!" I glanced at Susie, and she just hung her head in laughter. Joe came on up the hallway looking at me, smiling. "Yes, that is your son," I said, laughing like a hyena. One thing Rome understood, and that was that he knew he could go to his parents for anything he needed. Rome graduated from Rust and moved to Memphis where he worked for FedEx.

In 1992, Rome became sick with a rare form of cancer, and on August 3, 1992, he passed away. I don't think Susie ever got over his death. I say this because we could be just sitting in the driveway talking about one thing, and out of nowhere, she would just start talking about Rome. It was very hard for her losing her only son. Susie would always tell me that Rome loved people and loved life because he was so full of life himself.

Monique Brooks, Susie's baby girl, was just the apple of her parents' eyes. As a child, she made Susie very proud of the fact that she took on the piano and mastered it well. I think what surprised Susie even more was her daughter's singing. Susie purchased a piano, and they used to sing for hours in the living room as Monique played the songs. My brothers and I thought that Monique was a little spoiled, but what could you expect? She was the baby girl. One time, Susie dressed Monique in a beautiful red dress. That's when my brothers Glen and Fred walked through the house singing the Ohio Players' song "Fire" to tease Monique. I used to aggravate her another way when I helped her put on her coat. As she brought one arm down the sleeve, I would put my mouth at the end of the sleeve. When her baby fingers hit my lips, I would kiss her them. I drove her nuts, but I loved it. Later in her childhood, Monique became famous for participating in beauty pageants. She did really well, I might add. The one thing that made me feel so blessed as a person was when Monique told Susie that she always wanted to marry someone just like her Uncle Dennis. Susie told me this on several occasions, and I always felt that it was an honor knowing that Monique looked at me like that. After high school, Monique attended Southern Mississippi University. From there she moved to Atlanta and found her wonderful husband, Tony Montgomery. Monique also went to law school and became the first any only attorney in the family. Susie was so proud of baby girl. She told me that this was Monique most difficult challenge. "Dennis," Susie said, "law school was tough for Monique. It reminded me of you when you went to Officer Candidate School in the navy." I definitively could relate to that. Monique and her family now reside in Jackson, Mississippi. Susie always compared Monique to our mother, Sarah Mae Stallings, because she was always on the go. Susie once said, "Dennis, I should have named Monique Sarah after our mother because she has those same genes in her."

One thing that I found very unique about Susie and her children is that Susie actually followed in her children's footsteps in one venture—pledging a sorority or fraternity. Wanda pledged Delta Sigma Theta at Mississippi State. Romeo pledged Omega Si Phi at Rust College. Monique pledged Delta at Southern Mississippi. They all pledged before their mother made her choice to go Greek when she returned to college as an adult. Susie pledge the Columbus Mississippi chapter of Delta Sigma Theta.

It was just a bond with her children that I hadn't seen too often. I believe the bond with her children grew stronger in their later years. I think that was because of her sacrifice to raise my brothers and me. I could tell this by the way she talked to me about her children during our private conversations. She would explain to me what was going on their lives and their children's lives. It has always fascinated me how much she praised her children's successes in life. Despite the attention she gave to me and my brothers, Susie always reserved her number-one caring love for her flourishing and triumphant children, Wanda, Rome, and Monique.

Chapter 9

Reflections and Reverence

As I look back at the special relationship I had with my sister, Susie, I am reminded of the one thing she did for me that transcended every other thing in my life, and that was introducing me to Jesus Christ and his salvation. In the fall of 1985, I was at home preparing to enter Officer Candidate School in the US Navy. Susie and I were standing in the driveway as I was about to leave. With tears in her eyes, she placed her hand on my shoulder and said this to me: "Dennis, if things start to get a little too tough for you and you feel as if you are just not going to make it, fall on your knees and call on the name of Jesus, and he will make it better." Not thinking too much about it at the time, I responded, "I will, Baby Sister." While at Officer Candidate School, I was hit with some of the greatest academic challenges of my life. I kept failing no matter how hard I studied. One night, while I was sitting at my desk studying for a test, I started to shake and cry because I could not understand the subject matter. Then, at that moment, I heard Susie's voice saying, "Fall on your knees and call on the name of Jesus." I immediately got up and went to my knees at my bedside. I prayed for thirty minutes and asked Jesus for help. When I got up, I felt so different. I went back to studying the subject, and instantly my mind was free and clear. Everything began to make sense to me. I aced the test I took the next day with a grade of

100 percent! Not only that, I breezed through the final weeks of Officer Candidate School with ease. For the first time in my life, I had found Jesus and I understood what it meant to be saved. I owed it all to my sister Susie.

Susie Will Stallings Brooks has been an inspiration in my life since the day I was born. I believe that, in 1968, when my mother was on her deathbed and she made her request to Susie and Susie made that promise, the Holy Spirit came upon Susie to help her take on that incredible challenge. I know this because, in one of our private conversations, I made this statement to her: "Baby Sister, I want to thank you so much for taking us in and helping us. I don't know how you did what you did, but I am so happy that you helped me become the person that I am."

"Well, Dennis," she said, "I couldn't have done it without God's help. I owe everything to him, and I give him the glory."

Another thing that my brothers and I adored about my sister was her love for sports. Susie would sit in front of the television with us on Sundays and watch football. She knew more about sports than any of us. It seemed to me that, as Susie became more elderly, her love for sports grew immensely. As we became adults, she would just jump right into a sports conversation. "Dennis, did you watch *Mike and Mike* on ESPN today?" she would ask, smiling as she greeted me at the door. And Tiger Woods—Susie loved her some Tiger Woods—and the New York Yankees! To top it all off was the fact that she was right with us for our love for the Dallas Cowboys. Susie kept her television on ESPN all the time, and nobody dared to touch the remote to change it. I do believe it was a getaway for her.

Another of my favorite reflections of Susie was her motivation and dedication in acquiring her master's degree. This inspired me because, with all the time and effort she put in in raising us, she still accomplished this task with flying colors. I know it was frustrating for her during the process because she looked at me one night while she was doing her homework and made this statement: "School is for children." I smiled as I walked down the hall. Nevertheless, Susie once again prevailed.

Susie Will Stallings Brooks will always be, to me, the epitome of hard work, dedication, and knowledge of raising children. From my learning to read to becoming a college graduate, from my tour in the navy to my first corporate job, and from my marriage to the establishment of my family, Susie has been the source of my encouragement. God blessed her at a young age with wisdom and intelligence to have all the answers for eight children who had no mother or father in their lives. From the day our mother gave birth to us, Susie has been there for us, and she never once let us down. I thank God for Susie making that promise to our mother because, if she hadn't, my brothers and I would have been lost without the guidance of this extraordinary woman, this brave mentor in our lives, this magnificent woman we called Baby Sister.

Epilogue

Susie Will Stallings Brooks was my epic icon in my life. The things she did for me I will cherish for the rest of my life. I know all my other brothers and sisters feel the same way. Because of her unselfish sacrifices, I was able to achieve some outstanding things in my own ventures. She laid a strong solid foundation for me that I will forever be grateful for. To this day, I am so thankful for the many doors she opened for me. I am so obliged to her for the many incredible people who helped me along the way because they were associated with her. I think the greatest transformation that transpired in my young life, for which I am most grateful to Susie, was my success in education, which was due to her strict discipline. Some would think that her methods were unorthodox. I, on the other hand, thought they were nothing short of genius.

As long as I live, I will always remember some of Susie's most famous words, which I still repeat in my life today. Here are some of my favorites:

- The grade F stands for fool, and you don't have to go to school to be a fool!
- Don't find nothing!
- There is only one way to act, and that is the right way!
- Go somewhere, sit down and put a book in your hand, and *read!*
- There is nothing good out there in those streets!
- Friends? You don't need any friends. There are enough people in this house for you to play with!

I miss and love you so much, Susie Will Stallings Brooks. You are gone but clearly not forgotten. Your voice and words will always have my ear for the rest of my life.

Susie will still always be the one source of my understanding in everything I go through. Susie will always be a magnificent inspiration to me and all my other brothers and sisters. She was the greatest, and we all called her Baby Sister.

Printed in the United States
By Bookmasters